The Childcare Business Blueprint

How to Start, Build & Scale a Profitable Childcare Business

By

Valerie Chester

Dedication

This book is dedicated to my daughter—my miracle.

You are the reason everything started.

You are the reason I kept going on the days I felt like giving up.

You are the reason I learned what it truly means to protect, to fight, and to love without limits.

From the moment you came into this world, you changed my life in ways I could never fully explain.

You gave me purpose when I felt lost.

You gave me strength when I felt weak.

You gave me a reason to build something bigger than myself.

This journey, this business, this mission… it all started with you.

I also dedicate this to my son, Valen.

Though your time here was short, your life mattered.

You changed me in ways that will stay with me forever.

You taught me strength, even through pain.

You reminded me how precious life is and how deeply we are capable of loving.

You would have been 10 this year.

And not a day goes by that you are not with me in everything I do.

And to Justin—

You came into my life and became family.
I may not have given birth to you, but I helped raise you, and you will always be my son.
Watching you grow into the man you are today has been a blessing I will never take for granted.
You are a part of this journey, a part of this story, and a part of this family in every way that matters.

To every parent who has experienced loss, who has felt alone, who has had to find strength they didn't know they had…

This is for you too.

And to every childcare provider who shows up every day with love, patience, and dedication—

This work is not easy, but it matters.

Every child you care for, every life you touch, every safe space you create… it matters more than you know.

This book is for the children.
This book is for the families.

This book is for the ones who refuse to give up.

— Valerie

Table Of Contents

Prologue

The Day My Daughter Was Born

There are moments in life that divide everything into two parts: life before, and life after.

For me, that moment began during a pregnancy that doctors believed should never continue.

When I first learned I was pregnant, my life was already in a difficult season. Two years earlier, I had lost my mother. That loss left a space in my life that could never truly be filled. My mother had been the person I turned to for advice, comfort, and guidance. When she passed away, I suddenly found myself facing adulthood, and motherhood without the one person who would have known exactly what to say.

Pregnancy is supposed to be a time when women lean on their mothers. They ask questions, share fears, and look for reassurance.

I did not have that.

I had to figure everything out on my own.

From the very beginning, the pregnancy was complicated. Doctors were concerned about what they were seeing during early examinations. Appointment after appointment brought more uncertainty. Eventually, the conversations shifted—from cautious monitoring to something much heavier.

Medical professionals began suggesting that I should consider ending the pregnancy.

They believed my baby might have serious complications. They spoke about rare conditions, developmental concerns, and the possibility that my child might not survive long after birth. One of the most serious concerns was a large hole in her heart that showed up on the ultrasound.

Their tone was careful and clinical. They explained everything in terms of risk.

But I could not accept that.

Something inside me refused to let go of the child growing inside of me. I did not see statistics or probabilities, I saw my baby. I believed she deserved a chance to live.

Even when the doctors prepared me for the worst, my heart told me to keep going.

So I did.

Throughout the pregnancy, fear followed me everywhere. Every appointment carried new questions. Every ultrasound came with uncertainty. At the same time, I was learning how to prepare for motherhood completely on my own.

There was no support system surrounding me.
No mother to guide me.
No one to hold my hand through those moments.

Still, I kept going, because I had to.

As the months passed, the warnings did not stop. Doctors continued to tell me that my baby might not survive. They explained that even if she made it to birth, her chances of living could be extremely limited.

But I held on to hope.

When the day of delivery finally arrived, I felt a mixture of exhaustion, fear, and determination. I had carried this child through months of uncertainty. Now everything came down to one moment.

My daughter was born at just 1 pound, 13.5 ounces, and only 13 inches long.
The room went quiet.

She was not breathing.

Time felt like it stopped. I watched doctors and nurses move quickly, trying to bring her to life. Every warning I had heard came rushing back at once.

In that moment, I thought I was losing her.

And then something happened that I will never forget.

In the middle of that silence, I heard my mother's voice.

She had passed away two years earlier, yet I heard her as clearly as if she were standing beside me. It wasn't loud. It wasn't dramatic.

It was calm. Familiar.

And in the very next moment—

My daughter cried.

That sound changed everything.

The room shifted instantly. Doctors and nurses moved with urgency, now focused on stabilizing her. They were shocked. Some of them could not believe she was breathing at all, especially after what had been seen on the ultrasound.

They even called other doctors who were not there to tell them what had just happened.

My baby was alive.

But the fight was far from over.

She was rushed to the neonatal intensive care unit, where she would remain for the next three and a half months.

The NICU is a place filled with both hope and fear. Machines beep constantly. Doctors speak carefully. Every parent is holding on to faith, waiting for good news.

Multiple specialists were involved in my daughter's care. Her condition was so rare and serious that several doctors closely monitored her progress.

Every day was uncertain.

Some days brought hope.
Other days brought fear.

I spent countless hours sitting beside her, watching machines track her breathing and heart rate, praying she would keep fighting.

Then one day, I heard the words no parent is ever prepared for.

They told me she might only live for two days.

Two days.

I remember feeling like everything inside me collapsed. I had already fought so hard for her, how could I prepare myself to lose her?

But those two days passed.

Then another.

Then another.

And my daughter kept fighting.

Day by day, she proved them wrong.

While she was fighting for her life, I was learning what true strength really looked like.

Not the kind of strength people talk about—but the kind you are forced to find when you have no other choice.

Watching her changed me.

It changed how I saw children. It changed how I understood how vulnerable they are. Children depend on adults for everything. They cannot speak up for themselves. They rely on us to protect them, to care for them, and to advocate for them.

That realization stayed with me long after she finally came home.

She was still fragile. She still needed care.

But she was alive.

She was my miracle.

Looking back now, I can see that experience shaped the direction of my life. At the time, I didn't know I would build a career in childcare. I didn't know I would spend years creating safe environments for children and helping other providers do the same.

But the seed had already been planted.

The moment my daughter took her first breath changed everything.

It changed how I saw responsibility.
It changed how I understood protection.
It changed how I viewed the role adults play in a child's life.
I realized something that would stay with me forever:

Children deserve to be safe.

They deserve to be protected.

They deserve to be surrounded by people who truly care.

Years later, those beliefs grew into something much bigger than I ever imagined.

What started as one mother fighting for her daughter's life became a lifelong commitment to protecting children.

My daughter didn't just survive.

She gave me purpose.

She showed me what strength looks like before she could even speak. She taught me that children are resilient, valuable, and deserving of environments where they can grow and feel safe.

Because of her, I no longer saw childcare as just supervision.

I saw it as responsibility.

I saw it as leadership.

I saw it as purpose.

The day my daughter was born changed my life forever.

It was the day fear and faith met in the same room.

It was the day I witnessed a miracle.

And it was the day everything in my life began to make sense.

What I didn't know then…

was that moment would shape my entire future.

It would grow into Rising Stars Childcare.

And it all began…

on the day my daughter was born.

Who This Book Is For

This book was created for individuals who are serious about building a childcare business the right way.

It is for those who understand that childcare is more than just supervision…

it is structure, responsibility, and leadership.

This Book Is For You If:

- You want to start a daycare but don't know where to begin

- You are still researching and trying to understand how the childcare industry works

- You already have a childcare program but feel overwhelmed, underpaid, or unstructured

- You are caring for children but not running your program like a real business

- You struggle with pricing, policies, or consistency

- You want to build a childcare business that is professional and profitable

- You are tired of guessing and ready to build your business with clarity and structure

- You want to avoid costly mistakes that many providers make in the beginning

- You are ready to take your childcare business seriously

This Book Is Not For You If:

- You are looking for shortcuts or quick money

- You are not willing to follow structure, systems, and standards

- You want to operate without policies, organization, or accountability

- You are not ready to treat childcare like a real business

What You'll Gain From This Book

By the time you finish this book, you will have a clear understanding of:

- The different childcare business models and which one fits you

- How licensing and regulations actually work
- How to price your childcare program for profit

- What policies you need to protect your business

- How to build structure, systems, and daily operations

- How to position your childcare business for long-term success

A Final Word Before You Begin

If you are ready to stop guessing and start building your childcare business with structure, clarity, and confidence—

You are in the right place.

Introduction

Why This Book Exists

Every business has a starting point. Some begin with a business plan, a market opportunity, or a carefully calculated financial decision.

Mine did not.

My journey into childcare began with a mother's instinct, a broken heart, and a realization that changed the course of my life.

After my daughter finally came home from the hospital—following months in the NICU—life looked very different. She was still medically fragile and required extra care. But life does not pause for hardship. Bills still had to be paid. Responsibilities did not disappear.

Like many parents, I had to find a way to balance caring for my child while still providing for her.

That meant I had to return to work.

Leaving my daughter in someone else's care for the first time was one of the hardest decisions I had ever made. As a mother who had watched her child fight for survival, trusting someone else with her care did not come easily.

But I did what millions of parents do every day.

I searched for a daycare and I hoped.

At first, everything seemed normal. The environment looked acceptable. The staff appeared friendly. And like most parents, I wanted to believe that the people caring for my child truly cared about her.

But over time, something didn't feel right.

My daughter was the only Black child in that daycare. She also had special medical needs because of everything she had gone through. Instead of being treated with patience and understanding, I began noticing things that made me uncomfortable.

The way she was spoken to.
The way she was handled.
The lack of warmth in the environment.

As a mother, you know when something is wrong.
You can feel it.
You can see it.

You can sense it in your child.

And I saw it in mine.

I removed her from that daycare and searched for another option.

The second daycare seemed promising at first. I wanted it to work, I needed it to work. But within weeks, that same uneasy feeling returned.

Every morning, she cried when I dropped her off.
Every afternoon, she came home withdrawn.

She was unhappy.

Watching that broke me.

That was the moment I realized something many people don't openly talk about:

Not every childcare environment is built with the child's well-being at the center.

Some are underprepared.
Some are poorly structured.

Some are simply not designed to provide the level of care children truly deserve.

I knew I couldn't keep placing my daughter in environments where she didn't feel safe.

But I still had responsibilities.

And at the same time, life began to collapse in other areas.

The medical bills from her hospital stay became overwhelming. Months of NICU care, specialists, and treatments added up quickly. I had missed a significant amount of work while staying by her side.

The financial pressure became impossible to ignore.

Eventually, my home went into foreclosure.
I had to file for bankruptcy.

Those experiences are more than financial—they are emotional. They make you feel like everything around you is falling apart at once.

During that time, I felt completely alone.

I was raising a medically fragile child without support. I was navigating financial struggles. And I was trying to figure out how to build a stable future for both of us.

And then something unexpected happened.

I knew a woman who had earned her CDA and wanted to open a daycare. She had the training, but not the space. I had a home. At the time, it seemed like a simple solution to let her operate from my house while I continued working.

At least, that was the plan.

For the first month, I stayed at my job while the daycare ran in my home. But every evening when I came back, I noticed things that didn't sit right.

The structure was weak.
The environment lacked consistency.
The program felt unorganized.

And the children deserved better.

The more I observed, the more I realized I couldn't ignore it.

So I made a decision that surprised even me.

I fired everyone.

In that moment, I took control of the daycare myself.

I didn't have a perfect plan. I didn't have years of experience running a childcare program.

But I had something stronger:

A deep commitment to creating an environment where children were truly safe, supported, and cared for.

That decision changed everything.

What started as a temporary solution became something much bigger.

I began learning everything I could—policies, licensing, operations, structure. I studied what worked and what didn't. I paid attention to what separated strong childcare programs from struggling ones.

Over time, the program began to grow.

My background in accounting helped me build structure, manage finances, and create systems. I wasn't just building a nurturing environment—I was building a sustainable business.

Years passed.

What started in my home grew into something I could never have imagined.

Today, I have spent more than fifteen years in the childcare industry. I have built programs, mentored providers, and helped others create environments that truly support children and families.

And through all of that, I learned something important:

Good intentions are not enough.

Loving children is essential—but it is not the same as running a structured childcare business.

Without systems, policies, leadership, and financial planning, even the most passionate providers can become overwhelmed.

That's why I created the framework that guides my work today.

I call it the **STARS Method.**

The STARS Method is built on the core principles every childcare program needs to succeed. It focuses on creating structured environments where children are safe, staff are supported, and businesses can operate sustainably.

Throughout this book, I will share the lessons I've learned—both from success and from the mistakes that forced me to grow.

My goal is simple:

To help you avoid costly mistakes.

To help you build a childcare business that is structured, sustainable, and impactful.

This book will show you how to create a program that operates professionally from the start—how to build policies, structure your business, and price your services correctly.

But more than anything, it will help you create something that truly matters.

Because childcare is not just supervision.

It is protection.

It is leadership.

It is responsibility.

It is creating a space where children feel safe, valued, and cared for every single day.

And that mission…

is what has guided my work for the past fifteen years.

And it is the reason this book exists.

Part I: The Truth About Childcare

Chapter One

Loving Children Is Not a
Business Model

One of the most common things I hear from people who want to start a childcare program is a simple statement:

"I love children."

And honestly, that statement does matter. Anyone working with children should care deeply about them. Patience, compassion, and a genuine desire to help children grow are essential qualities in this field. Without those qualities, childcare becomes just another job, and children deserve far more than that.

But over the years, I have learned something that surprises many new providers:

Loving children is not a business model.

It may be the reason someone feels drawn to this work, but it is not enough to sustain a childcare program long term. Passion alone cannot replace planning, structure, financial awareness, and leadership. Without those elements, even the most well-inattention childcare providers eventually find themselves overwhelmed.

Many people enter the childcare field with their hearts in the right place, but without a clear understanding of what running a childcare program actually involves.

They imagine spending their days teaching, playing with children, and creating a nurturing environment. What they do not always see ahead of time are the operational responsibilities that come with it:

- Scheduling
- Policies
- Financial management
- Licensing regulations
- Communication with families
- Safety procedures
- Staff supervision

Running a childcare program means managing all of these responsibilities at the same time while still providing high-quality care for children every day.

Without preparation, that balance can become incredibly difficult.

The Difference
Between Passion and Structure

Passion is the emotional drive that brings people into childcare. Structure is what allows them to stay in the industry long enough to make a real impact.

In the early stages of starting a childcare program, passion often leads providers to make decisions based on feelings rather than strategy. They want to help families. They want to be flexible. They want to make things easier for parents who are already juggling work and family life.

Those intentions come from a good place. But when they are not balanced with clear policies and boundaries, they can quickly create problems.

For example, many new providers hesitate to charge what their services are truly worth. They worry that parents may not be able to afford the tuition or that raising prices might make families uncomfortable.

So they lower their rates.

At first, it feels like a generous decision. But over time, the financial reality begins to show. Operating a childcare program comes with significant expenses. Food, educational materials, insurance, licensing fees, supplies, and facility costs all add up.

When tuition rates are set too low, providers eventually find themselves working long hours without the financial stability they expected.

Passion alone cannot cover operational expenses.

Another example appears in the area of policies. New providers often want to seem flexible and understanding. They hesitate to enforce strict policies because they want parents to feel comfortable.

But without clear policies, situations quickly become inconsistent.

One parent might arrive late for pick-up without consequences. Another might delay tuition payments. Over time, those small exceptions add up, creating an environment where the provider feels constantly pressured to make emotional decisions rather than structured ones.

Eventually, the workload and stress begin to build.

Learning Through Experience

When I first began running my childcare program, I made many of the same mistakes that new providers make today. At the time, I did not fully understand how important structure would become in maintaining a stable environment.

One of my earliest mistakes involved pricing.

When I set my tuition rates, I was thinking primarily about the families I wanted to serve. I knew many parents struggled to find affordable childcare, and I wanted to make my program accessible.

So I priced my services too low.

At first, the decision seemed reasonable. Families were grateful for the affordable option, and enrollment filled quickly. But as the months passed, the financial pressure became obvious.

The cost of operating the program continued to rise. Food, supplies, learning materials, and licensing expenses all required consistent funding. Because my tuition rates were too low, there was very little margin to reinvest in the program.

I was working long hours and carrying a heavy responsibility, yet the financial stability I expected was not there.

Eventually, I had to reevaluate my pricing structure entirely.

That experience taught me an important lesson: childcare providers must understand the true value of the service they offer. Caring for children is one of the most important responsibilities a person can have, and the business side of that work must reflect its value.

Another mistake I made early on involved policies.

When parents approached me with requests or challenges, I often responded emotionally. If a parent explained that they were struggling financially that week, I might allow a delayed payment. If someone arrived late for pick-up, I might overlook the policy I had written down.

At the time, I believed I was being compassionate.

What I did not realize was that inconsistent enforcement creates confusion. When policies are not applied equally, expectations become unclear for everyone involved.

Over time, I began noticing that the same situations repeated themselves more frequently. Parents assumed flexibility would always be available because it had been allowed before.

That is when I began to understand that policies are not meant to create distance between providers and families. They exist to create fairness and stability.

Once I started enforcing policies consistently, the entire program became easier to manage:

- Parents knew what to expect
- Schedules became more predictable
- Stress levels decreased

Structure allowed the program to operate more smoothly.

The Hidden Demands of Childcare

Many people underestimate how demanding the childcare profession can be. On the surface, it may appear similar to babysitting. But operating a childcare program requires far more responsibility than most people initially expect.

Providers are responsible for supervising multiple children at the same time, often with different developmental needs and personalities. They must maintain safe environments while guiding learning activities, managing behavioral challenges, and communicating with parents.

At the same time, they must manage the operational side of the business.

- Paperwork must be completed
- Schedules must be organized
- Supplies must be purchased
- Licensing requirements must be met

The work does not end when the last child leaves for the day. Many providers spend their evenings preparing lesson plans, organizing materials, and handling administrative tasks that keep the program running.

Without proper systems in place, this workload can quickly become overwhelming.

That is one of the main reasons burnout occurs so frequently in the childcare industry.

Providers enter the field because they care deeply about children. But when the operational demands grow beyond what they expected, the emotional and physical exhaustion becomes difficult to sustain.

Burnout does not happen because providers stop caring. It happens because the structure needed to support the work was never fully established.

Building a Sustainable Program

Over time, I learned that running a successful childcare program requires balancing two important priorities.

The first priority is the well-being of the children. Every decision should ultimately support their safety, development, and emotional security.

The second priority is the stability of the program itself.

If the program is not financially sustainable, properly structured, and well organized, it becomes difficult to maintain the level of care children deserve.

These two priorities must work together.

Clear policies help maintain fairness and organization. Proper pricing ensures that the program can continue operating and improving over time. Structured routines help children feel secure while allowing providers to manage their responsibilities effectively.

When these elements are in place, childcare providers are able to focus on the most rewarding parts of their work.

They can build relationships with families.

They can support children's learning and growth.

They can create environments where children feel safe and valued.

But without structure, those goals become much harder to achieve.

A New Way to Think About Childcare

The longer I worked in this field, the more clearly I understood something that many new providers do not realize when they first begin:

Childcare is both a calling and a business.

It requires compassion, patience, and dedication. But it also requires planning, systems, and leadership. When providers treat childcare as a professional operation rather than simply a passion project, the results are dramatically different.

- Programs become more stable
- Families receive more consistent care
- Children benefit from well-organized environments

And providers themselves are able to build careers that are sustainable rather than exhausting.

That shift in perspective changed the way I approached my own program. Instead of making decisions based only on emotion, I began building systems that supported both the children and the business itself.

The results transformed everything.

Loving children is the reason many people enter the childcare profession. It is the foundation of the work, and it should never be lost.

But love alone cannot support the weight of an entire childcare program.

Without structure, planning, and clear systems, even the most passionate provider will eventually struggle to maintain balance.

Childcare must be approached as a professional operation. It requires thoughtful pricing, clear policies, organized routines, and strong leadership.

When those elements are in place, providers are able to create environments where children truly thrive.

And that is when childcare becomes more than just a passion.

It becomes a sustainable and meaningful business.

Chapter Two

The Childcare Industry No One
Talks About

From the outside, childcare can appear simple.

To many people, it looks like a room full of toys, a few teachers guiding activities, and children spending their day playing while their parents are at work. Because of that surface-level image, childcare is often misunderstood. People assume the work is easy, informal, and not particularly demanding.

But anyone who has spent time inside a childcare program knows that this perception could not be further from the truth.

Behind the cheerful classrooms and daily routines lies one of the most demanding professions a person can enter. Childcare providers carry immense responsibility every day, yet the depth of that responsibility is rarely recognized by the public.

The reality is that childcare is not simply about supervising children while their parents are away.

It is about shaping early development, managing environments, protecting safety, guiding emotional growth, and supporting families who rely on these programs to function in their daily lives.

Every decision a childcare provider makes can influence a child's experience during some of the most important developmental years of their life.

Despite this responsibility, the industry itself often receives far less professional respect than it deserves.

When Childcare Is Viewed as Babysitting

One of the most persistent challenges in the childcare field is how the work is perceived by people outside the profession.

In many communities, childcare is still treated as if it is simply an extension of babysitting. The assumption is that providers are mainly responsible for watching children until their parents return.

Because of this, the skill and training involved in early childhood care are often overlooked.

The difference between babysitting and childcare, however, is significant.

Babysitting is typically temporary and informal. It usually takes place for short periods of time, often within a family's home, and focuses mainly on keeping children safe while parents are away.

Professional childcare programs operate very differently.

A childcare provider is responsible not only for safety, but also for creating an environment where children learn structure, build social skills, and develop emotional awareness. Providers guide children through routines that help them understand cooperation, communication, and self-regulation. They introduce activities that stimulate curiosity and encourage learning in ways that are appropriate for each stage of development.

These early experiences shape how children interact with others and how they approach learning as they grow.

Because these responsibilities are so important, professional childcare requires far more preparation than many people realize. Providers must understand child development, safety procedures, communication strategies, and behavior management. They must also follow licensing regulations designed to protect children and ensure programs operate responsibly.

Yet even with all of these responsibilities, childcare providers often face the challenge of being treated as though their work requires little expertise.

Parents may question tuition rates while overlooking the operational costs involved in maintaining a safe and structured environment. Communities may speak about the importance of early childhood education without recognizing the professionals who deliver it.

This gap between responsibility and recognition is one of the reasons many childcare providers feel undervalued.

The Emotional Side of the Work

Another aspect of childcare that is rarely discussed openly is the emotional commitment required to do the work well.

Children bring their entire world into a childcare environment each day. They arrive with different personalities, moods, and experiences from home. Some are excited and energetic. Others may feel shy, anxious, or overwhelmed by the separation from their parents.

A skilled childcare provider learns how to respond to each of those emotions with patience and understanding.

For a young child, even small events can feel overwhelming. A disagreement with a friend, frustration during an activity, or difficulty expressing feelings can quickly lead to tears or emotional outbursts.

In those moments, the provider becomes the steady presence that helps the child regain a sense of calm and safety.

This type of support requires emotional energy throughout the entire day.

Providers must remain patient even when several children need attention at once. They must maintain a calm tone when guiding children through challenging situations. They must offer reassurance to children who are learning how to navigate the world around them.

At the same time, providers are communicating with parents, answering questions, and addressing concerns about each child's progress and well-being.

Balancing all of these responsibilities requires not only skill, but emotional resilience.

The emotional side of childcare is deeply rewarding, but without the right systems and support, it can also become exhausting.

The Challenge of Staffing

As childcare programs grow, another challenge becomes more visible: staffing.

Finding and retaining qualified staff members is one of the most difficult aspects of running a childcare program. The work requires patience, responsibility, and genuine care for children, yet compensation within the industry often does not reflect the level of responsibility involved.

Because of this, many programs experience frequent turnover.

A teacher may begin working in childcare with enthusiasm but eventually move to another field that offers higher pay or more predictable hours. When that happens, the program must begin the hiring and training process again.

Each transition affects both the program and the children.

Children build relationships with the adults who care for them daily. When a teacher leaves, children must adjust to a new person guiding their routines and activities. For program leaders, each staffing change requires time spent interviewing, onboarding, and supporting new employees while maintaining the quality of care families expect.

When a program is short-staffed, the remaining team members often take on additional responsibilities. Over time, this increases stress and makes an already demanding job even more challenging.

The Length of the Workday

Another reality that people outside the childcare field rarely see is the length of the workday.

Most childcare programs open early in the morning to accommodate working parents. Some begin welcoming children before sunrise, while others remain open well into the evening. Providers often work ten to twelve hours a day to meet the needs of families.

Throughout those hours, the pace rarely slows.

Children require constant supervision, guidance, and engagement. Activities must be organized, meals prepared, and routines maintained. Providers are responsible for ensuring that each child remains safe while also creating an environment that encourages exploration and learning.

And once the children leave, the work is not always finished.

Classrooms must be cleaned and prepared for the next day. Lesson plans need to be organized. Administrative responsibilities such as documentation, communication with families, and regulatory requirements still require attention.

Without strong systems in place, the workday extends far beyond operating hours.

When Burnout Begins to Appear

Over time, the combination of long hours, emotional responsibility, and operational demands can begin to take a toll.

Burnout does not usually happen suddenly. It develops gradually when the daily demands of the work begin to outweigh the systems in place to support it.

A provider may begin their career with enthusiasm and dedication. They enjoy building relationships with children and families. They take pride in creating a safe and nurturing environment.

But as time passes, the responsibilities continue to grow.

Financial pressures increase. Staffing challenges add to the workload. The emotional commitment remains constant.

Without clear boundaries, structured policies, and sustainable systems, providers can begin to feel physically and emotionally drained.

This is one of the most difficult realities of the childcare industry, because the people experiencing burnout are often the ones who care the most.

Why Many Programs Close Within the First Five Years

Across the childcare industry, it is common to see programs open with excitement and close just a few years later.

The first year often feels promising. Families enroll, routines are established, and relationships begin to grow. The program appears successful.

But over time, certain challenges begin to surface.

One of the most common issues is financial miscalculation. Many providers underestimate the true cost of operating a childcare business. They set tuition rates based on what they believe families can afford rather than what the business actually requires to operate sustainably.

Expenses such as supplies, insurance, licensing fees, maintenance, and food costs add up quickly. Without careful planning, providers may find themselves working long hours without financial stability.

Another factor is the absence of clear operational structure.

When policies are weak or inconsistently enforced, providers find themselves constantly reacting to problems instead of preventing them. Late payments, schedule changes, and unclear expectations create ongoing stress that slowly drains energy from the program.

Staffing challenges also play a role. Programs that rely on employees must maintain consistent staffing levels to meet safety regulations. When turnover is high or qualified candidates are difficult to find, maintaining stability becomes much more complicated.

But perhaps the most significant factor is burnout.

Providers who enter the industry with passion but without long-term structure often become overwhelmed by the demands of running the program.

Eventually, some reach a point where they decide they can no longer continue.

Understanding the Industry Honestly

Discussing these challenges is not meant to discourage anyone from entering the childcare profession. In fact, understanding these realities is one of the most important steps toward building a program that lasts.

Childcare is essential to every community. Families rely on it in order to work and provide for their households. Children benefit from environments where they are guided by adults who care about their development and well-being.

But for childcare programs to truly thrive, they must be built on strong foundations.

Providers must recognize that they are not simply offering supervision. They are creating environments that influence the early stages of human development.

That level of responsibility requires preparation, structure, and professionalism.

When childcare providers approach their work with both passion and business awareness, the results are powerful.

- Programs become more stable
- Families feel confident in the care their children receive

- Providers build careers that are both meaningful and sustainable

The childcare industry may not always receive the recognition it deserves, but the impact of the work happening within it is undeniable.

And when the profession is approached with the seriousness it deserves, childcare becomes far more than a service.

It becomes a foundation for the future.

Chapter Three

Why Structure Protects Children

When people think about childcare, they usually think about warmth, patience, and compassion. Those qualities are important, and every strong childcare provider should possess them. Children thrive when they feel cared for, respected, and emotionally supported by the adults around them.

But there is another element of childcare that is just as important yet talked about far less often:

Structure

Structure is what transforms a childcare environment from a loosely organized space into a safe, dependable system where children can grow and develop with confidence.

Without structure, even the most caring provider can struggle to maintain consistency, safety, and stability. With structure, a childcare program becomes a place where both children and adults understand expectations, routines, and responsibilities.

In many ways, structure is the invisible framework that holds a childcare program together. It shapes how decisions are made, how responsibilities are handled, and how the environment operates every single day.

Most importantly, structure protects children.

The Role of Policies In Protecting Children

One of the clearest ways structure shows up in a childcare program is through policies.

Policies are often misunderstood by new providers because they can seem strict or overly formal. Some worry that policies will make their program feel rigid or impersonal.

In reality, well-designed policies do the opposite they create clarity, fairness, and safety.

When a childcare program has clear policies in place, families understand expectations from the very beginning. Arrival times, pick-up procedures, illness guidelines, and communication standards are all established before problems arise.

This reduces confusion and allows providers to focus on caring for children rather than constantly resolving misunderstandings.

Policies also play a critical role in safety.

Authorized pick-up procedures ensure that children are only released to approved individuals. Illness policies help prevent the spread of contagious conditions. Emergency procedures prepare staff to respond quickly and effectively when unexpected situations occur.

Without these systems, providers are forced to make decisions in the moment without clear guidance. That kind of uncertainty increases risk.

When policies are thoughtfully written and consistently enforced, they create a protective boundary around the program. They ensure decisions are based on established standards—not emotion or convenience.

Training as a Foundation for Safety

Another essential component of structure in childcare is training.

Caring for children requires far more than supervision. Providers must understand child development, recognize behavioral cues, maintain safe environments, and respond appropriately in emergencies.

These responsibilities require preparation.

Training provides the knowledge and skills needed to handle the wide range of situations that occur in a childcare setting. First aid and CPR training ensure providers can respond to medical emergencies. Child development education helps them understand age-appropriate behaviors and guide children effectively.

Beyond practical skills, training builds confidence.

When staff members understand why procedures exist, they are more likely to follow them consistently. And consistency is critical in childcare environments where multiple adults share responsibility.

When everyone is trained the same way, the program operates with alignment.

Children benefit from that consistency. They experience the same expectations, routines, and responses regardless of which staff member is present. That predictability helps them feel secure and supported.

Without proper training, even well-meaning providers may struggle in challenging situations.

Training gives them the tools to protect and guide children effectively.

The Importance of Leadership

Structure within a childcare program depends heavily on leadership.

Every successful program has someone responsible for guiding the overall direction of the environment—whether that is an owner, director, or lead provider.

Leadership in childcare goes beyond managing daily operations. It involves setting clear expectations, communicating effectively, and ensuring that the program's standards are consistently upheld.

A strong leader reinforces both safety and professionalism.

They ensure policies are followed. They support staff members. They address challenges early instead of allowing them to grow into larger problems.

While children may not always recognize leadership directly, they experience the results of it every day.

When leadership is strong, the environment feels calm, organized, and predictable. Staff members understand their roles, and families feel confident in the care their children receive.

Without leadership, even well-designed systems begin to break down.

Policies become inconsistent. Expectations become unclear. Small issues turn into larger problems.

Leadership keeps the structure intact.

The Value of Predictable Environments

Children naturally respond to environments that feel predictable and organized.

While adults may appreciate flexibility and spontaneity, young children feel most secure when their daily routines follow a consistent pattern.

In a structured childcare program, children know what to expect.

They understand when it is time for meals, activities, rest, and play. These routines help them transition smoothly throughout the day and reduce anxiety that can come from uncertainty.

Structure also supports learning.

When children feel secure in their environment, they are more open to exploring new ideas, engaging with others, and participating in activities.

For example, clearly defined areas within a classroom help children understand how the space is used. One area may be for reading, another for creative play, and another for hands-on learning.

These simple structures build confidence and independence.

It is important to understand that structure does not limit creativity—it supports it.

When routines are organized and expectations are clear, providers have more time and energy to focus on meaningful, engaging experiences.

Without structure, the environment can quickly become chaotic.

Transitions become difficult. Expectations become unclear. And children may feel less secure.

Structure creates the conditions where both safety and learning can thrive.

Connecting Structure and Safety

When people think about safety, they often focus on physical measures like locked doors, safety gates, or secure equipment.

While those are important, true safety in childcare goes much deeper.

Safety comes from systems.

- Policies create consistent expectations.
- Training ensures proper responses.
- Leadership provides accountability.
- Routines create predictability.

Together, these elements form the structure of the program.

When structure is in place, providers can anticipate challenges and prevent problems before they happen.

Without structure, providers are constantly reacting instead of leading.

In childcare, preparation is one of the strongest forms of protection.

Children rely on adults to create environments where they can explore safely. Structure makes that possible.

Structure as a Professional Standard

One of the most important mindset shifts for childcare providers is understanding that structure is not a limitation.

It is a professional standard.

When providers build programs with clear systems and expectations, they create environments where everyone benefits.

Staff members feel supported because they understand how the program operates. Families feel confident because they see consistency and professionalism.

Over time, this builds trust within the community.

Parents recommend programs they trust. Staff stay in environments where expectations are clear. Programs become more stable and respected.

Structure strengthens every part of the business.

The Core Principle

At the heart of every successful childcare program is a simple but powerful truth:

The structure of the business directly influences the safety of the children within it.

When policies are clear, staff are trained, leadership is strong, and routines are consistent, children benefit from an environment designed to protect and support them.

Without those systems, even the most caring provider may struggle to maintain stability.

Childcare is built on compassion, patience, and dedication.

But those qualities must be supported by structure.

Because in the end, structure is not about control.

It is about responsibility.

And in childcare, responsibility always begins with protecting the children entrusted to your care.

Part II: Building Your Foundation

Chapter Four

The Six Childcare Business Models

When people decide to start a childcare program, one of the first questions they usually ask is:

"Where do I begin?"

Many assume the answer is simply to open a daycare and start enrolling children. But in reality, the first and most important decision happens even earlier.

You must decide what type of childcare business you are building.

The childcare industry includes several different business models, each with its own requirements, startup costs, regulations, and lifestyle implications. Some are designed for small home-based environments, while others operate as full-scale childcare centers serving large numbers of families.

Understanding these models before you begin is critical because the structure you choose will influence almost every part of your business.

It determines:

- How much money you need to start
- How many children you can serve
- What licensing is required
- What your daily schedule will look like

Some models offer flexibility but limit growth. Others provide higher income potential but require larger investments and more complex management.

Choosing the right model is not just about income—it is about the lifestyle and work environment you want to create.

Licensed Home Daycare

One of the most common entry points into the childcare industry is the licensed home daycare.

This model allows providers to operate a childcare program from their residence while meeting state licensing requirements.

Licensed home daycares are typically smaller programs, often serving between six and twelve children depending on regulations, ages, and whether assistants are present.

Because the program operates in a home, startup costs are generally lower than opening a childcare center. However, providers must still meet safety requirements such as childproofing, installing gates, and creating designated learning areas. Licensing inspections ensure the environment meets health and safety standards.

One of the biggest advantages of this model is flexibility.

Providers can often create their own schedules and build a more personal environment where children receive individual attention.

However, this also means the provider carries full responsibility.

They manage:
- Supervision
- Meals
- Cleaning
- Curriculum
- Parent communication
- Daily operations

Income is limited by capacity, so pricing must be set carefully to ensure sustainability.

For those who prefer a smaller, relationship-based environment, this model can be both manageable and rewarding.

Unlicensed Home Daycare

Some providers begin by operating a home-based childcare program without obtaining a license.

However, regulations for unlicensed care vary by state. In some areas, providers may legally care for a small number of children without licensing. In others, operating without a license may not be permitted beyond a certain point.

Because of this, it is essential to understand your local laws before choosing this path.

Unlicensed home daycares often have very low startup costs and can begin with a small group of children from a personal network or community.

However, this model comes with limitations.

Many families prefer licensed programs because licensing provides reassurance that safety standards have been met. Without that credibility, it may be more difficult to build trust or grow enrollment.

In addition, capacity is usually restricted, which limits income potential.

Some providers use this model as a starting point before becoming licensed. Others intentionally remain small and informal.

The key to this model is operating responsibly while staying within legal boundaries.

Licensed Childcare Centers

Licensed childcare centers represent one of the most structured and scalable models in the industry.

Unlike home-based programs, centers operate in commercial facilities designed to serve larger groups of children.

Opening a childcare center requires a significant investment.

Startup costs may include:
- Leasing or purchasing a building
- Renovations to meet licensing standards
- Equipment and materials
- Hiring and training staff

Because of these costs, careful financial planning is essential.

However, the growth potential is much higher.

Centers can serve dozens or even hundreds of children depending on size and staffing. This allows for significantly higher revenue when managed properly.

Licensed centers must comply with strict regulations, including:

- Staff-to-child ratios
- Training requirements
- Safety procedures
- Facility standards

Managing a center also requires strong leadership.

Owners and directors must oversee staff, manage finances, maintain compliance, and ensure high-quality care.

While the responsibility is greater, successful centers play a major role in supporting families and communities.

Unlicensed Childcare Centers

In some areas, smaller group programs may operate in commercial spaces without being classified as fully licensed childcare centers.

These programs often exist under alternative regulations based on size, hours, or age groups served.

However, this model can be risky.

It often operates in a legal gray area, and regulations can change quickly. Programs that grow beyond certain limits may be required to become licensed.

Because of this, many providers eventually transition into licensed centers to build long-term stability and credibility.

Families are increasingly aware of licensing standards, and licensed programs tend to attract more trust and consistent enrollment.

If considering this model, it is critical to fully understand state regulations and ensure compliance.

Ministry Childcare

Ministry-based childcare programs are typically operated by churches or faith-based organizations.

These programs often serve as part of a community outreach effort.

In some states, ministry childcare operates under different regulatory structures than traditional childcare centers. While safety standards still apply, licensing requirements may differ.

Regulations vary by state, so it is important to understand how these programs are defined locally.

One major advantage is lower startup costs.

Churches often already have:
- Classrooms
- Kitchens
- Play areas

This reduces the need for building or leasing a new facility.

Ministry programs also benefit from strong community trust, especially among families connected to the organization.

However, they still require proper management, trained staff, and structured systems to ensure quality care.

After-School and School-Age Programs

Another important segment of childcare focuses on school-age children.

After-school programs provide supervision and structured activities once the school day ends.

These programs typically operate for a few hours in the afternoon and may include:

- Homework support
- Recreational activities
- Social development opportunities

Because of shorter hours, these programs often require:

- Fewer staff
- Lower startup costs

They can operate in:

- Schools
- Community centers
- Churches
- Childcare facilities

Some programs also expand to include summer camps or holiday care.

Income depends on enrollment and pricing, but the ability to serve larger groups can increase revenue.

One key consideration is scheduling.

These programs follow the academic calendar, which means operations may fluctuate throughout the year.

Despite this, they provide an essential service for working families.

Choosing the Right Model

Each childcare business model comes with its own opportunities and challenges.

- Home daycares offer flexibility and personal environments but limit growth
- Childcare centers offer scalability but require larger investments
- Ministry and after-school programs provide alternative structures based on community needs

The best model depends on:

- Your financial resources

- Local regulations
- Long-term goals
- Desired lifestyle

Some providers start with home-based programs and expand over time. Others choose to remain small and relationship-focused.

What matters most is choosing a structure that allows you to build a program that is both effective and sustainable.

A childcare business is not simply about opening a space.

It is about creating a system that can operate consistently while providing safe, structured, and supportive environments for children and families.

Understanding the different models available is the first step toward building that system successfully.

Chapter Five

Understanding Licensing and Regulations

For many people who want to start a childcare program, licensing is one of the first topics that creates uncertainty.

Some hear stories about complicated paperwork, strict inspections, or long approval processes and begin to wonder whether licensing is something to avoid altogether.

Others assume that licensing is simply a bureaucratic step designed to create extra work.

Both of these perspectives miss the larger purpose behind licensing.

Licensing is not designed to make childcare more difficult. It exists to protect children and to support providers in creating environments that meet clear safety and operational standards.

When childcare programs follow licensing requirements, families gain confidence that their children are in environments designed to prioritize their well-being.

Understanding how licensing works is essential for anyone planning to operate a childcare business. It provides the framework that ensures programs are not only nurturing, but also safe, responsible, and professionally managed.

The Myths Surrounding Licensing

One of the most common misconceptions about licensing is that it is impossible to navigate without legal expertise or specialized experience.

New providers often imagine a long, complicated process filled with confusing regulations.

In reality, most licensing systems are designed to guide providers step by step.

Each state has a licensing agency responsible for overseeing childcare programs. These agencies typically offer:

- Clear instructions
- Orientation sessions
- Training materials
- Support throughout the process

While licensing does require preparation and attention to detail, it is not meant to prevent people from entering the field.

Another common myth is that inspections exist to punish providers.

Many new applicants worry that inspectors are looking for reasons to deny applications or shut down programs.

In reality, inspectors are there to ensure safety standards are met.

They identify areas for improvement and help providers understand how to meet requirements. When approached correctly, inspections become part of building a strong program not something to fear.

Some providers also believe that staying unlicensed allows them to avoid regulations entirely.

However, operating outside the licensing system often leads to:
- Limited enrollment capacity
- Reduced trust from families
- Legal risks depending on the state

Licensing, when understood properly, becomes an advantage—not an obstacle.

Background Checks and Protecting Children

One of the most important components of licensing is background screening.

Because childcare providers work closely with children, licensing agencies require thorough checks to ensure that anyone responsible for care has been properly vetted.

These checks often include:
- Criminal background history
- Fingerprinting
- Child abuse registry screenings

While this process may feel intrusive, it serves a critical purpose.

Parents trust childcare providers with their children's safety. Knowing that every adult in a licensed program has been screened builds that trust.

In home-based childcare, this requirement often extends beyond the provider.

Any adult living in the home may also need to complete background checks to ensure the environment is safe.

These measures create an additional layer of protection for both children and providers.

Safety Standards in Childcare Environments

Licensing regulations also establish safety standards for the physical environment.

These standards cover everything from building conditions to daily routines.

Childcare spaces must be designed to minimize risk.

Examples include:
- Covered electrical outlets
- Secured cleaning supplies
- Safe and age-appropriate play areas

Outdoor spaces must also meet safety guidelines to prevent injuries.

Fire safety is another key component.

Programs are typically required to have:
- Smoke detectors
- Fire extinguishers
- Emergency evacuation plans

- Regular safety drills

Sanitation standards are equally important.

Providers must follow procedures for:
- Handwashing
- Food preparation
- Diapering
- Cleaning toys and surfaces

These details exist for a simple reason:

Young children are still learning how to navigate the world safely. Their environments must be designed to protect them.

Understanding Child-to-Staff Ratios

Child-to-staff ratios are another critical part of licensing.

These ratios determine how many children each adult can supervise.

The purpose is simple: safety and quality care.

When too many children are assigned to one adult, supervision decreases and risks increase.

Licensing agencies set ratios based on age groups.

- Infants and toddlers require more supervision
- Older children can be in slightly larger groups

For providers, understanding ratios is essential when planning enrollment and staffing.

While ratios may seem limiting, they actually improve the quality of care.

Smaller group sizes allow providers to:
- Give more attention
- Build stronger relationships
- Support development more effectively

The Role of Inspections

Licensing inspections are an ongoing part of maintaining a childcare program.

These inspections may occur before opening and periodically throughout the year.

Inspectors review:
- Safety conditions
- Documentation
- Staff qualifications
- Policy compliance

For new providers, inspections can feel intimidating.
But they are not designed to create fear.

They are designed to maintain standards.

Programs that stay organized, follow procedures, and maintain documentation often find inspections to be straightforward.

Inspections also provide reassurance to families that the program is being monitored and maintained at a professional level.

Insurance and Financial Protection

Licensing often includes requirements related to insurance.

Operating a childcare business comes with responsibility, and insurance helps protect both providers and families.

The most common type is liability insurance.

This covers the program in case of accidents or injuries.

Additional coverage may include:
- Property insurance
- Business operation coverage

While no provider expects something to go wrong, insurance ensures that the program is prepared if it does.

It is a key part of operating responsibly.

Why Licensing Matters

When all of these elements are considered together—background checks, safety standards, ratios, inspections, and insurance—the purpose of licensing becomes clear.

Licensing creates a structured system that protects children while supporting providers.

Families benefit because they know their children are in safe, regulated environments.

Providers benefit because clear standards create organization, reduce risk, and build trust.

Successful childcare providers do not view licensing as a barrier.

They see it as a foundation.

It establishes expectations, strengthens operations, and reinforces professionalism.

Childcare is one of the most important services a community can offer. Parents rely on providers to protect and nurture their children every day.

Licensing helps ensure that responsibility is carried out with the level of care it deserves.

For anyone entering the childcare field, understanding licensing is not just about following rules.

It is about embracing a system designed to safeguard the children who depend on you every day.

Chapter Six

Pricing Your Childcare Program Correctly

One of the most important decisions a childcare provider will ever make is how to price their program. It is also one of the areas where many providers make costly mistakes, especially in the early stages of their business.

Pricing is often approached with good intentions. Providers want to help families, remain affordable, and fill their enrollment quickly. They look at what others in their area are charging and try to position themselves as the more "reasonable" option.

At first, this may seem like a smart strategy.

Lower prices can attract families quickly and create the appearance of demand. Enrollment may grow, classrooms may fill, and the program may feel successful on the surface.

But over time, a different reality begins to emerge.

Expenses increase. Responsibilities grow. And despite working long hours, the financial return does not match the level of effort required to sustain the program.

This is where many childcare businesses begin to struggle—not because there is no demand, but because the pricing structure was never built to support the business long term.

Understanding how to price a childcare program correctly is not simply about choosing a number. It is about building a financial foundation that allows the program to operate sustainably while maintaining high-quality care.

Why Many Providers Underprice

Underpricing is one of the most common patterns in the childcare industry, and it usually begins with emotion rather than strategy.

Many providers enter childcare because they genuinely care about children and families. They understand that parents are balancing multiple responsibilities and do not want to add financial pressure by charging higher rates.

While this mindset is compassionate, it can lead to unsustainable decisions.

Instead of calculating what it truly costs to operate the program, providers often base their pricing on what they believe families can afford or what feels comfortable to charge. Some also look at competitors who are already underpricing and attempt to match or go lower to remain competitive.

Over time, this creates a cycle where pricing across the market becomes disconnected from the actual cost of providing care.

Fear also plays a role.

Providers worry that higher tuition will drive families away or make enrollment more difficult. However, pricing too low creates a different type of instability—one that places constant pressure on the provider.

When tuition does not cover expenses, providers are forced to work longer hours, reduce investments in their program, or operate under ongoing financial stress.

This is not sustainable.

The Problem with Emotional Pricing

Emotional pricing occurs when tuition decisions are based on feelings rather than facts.

It often appears in small ways.

A provider may lower a rate for one family out of sympathy. They may allow late payments without consequence. They may delay raising tuition even as costs increase.

Individually, these decisions may seem minor.

But over time, they weaken the financial structure of the entire program.

When pricing becomes inconsistent, fairness becomes unclear. Some families may pay different rates for the same service, and informal agreements become difficult to track.

More importantly, emotional pricing makes it nearly impossible to plan ahead.

A childcare business must operate with predictable income in order to remain stable. Providers need to understand how much revenue is coming in and how it aligns with expenses.

Without that clarity, the business becomes reactive instead of intentional.

Establishing firm pricing is not about being rigid or uncaring. It is about creating a system that allows the program to continue operating without constant financial strain.

Understanding the Real Cost of Childcare

Before setting tuition, providers must understand the true cost of operating their program.

Many new providers focus only on visible expenses such as food or supplies. While important, these represent only part of the overall financial picture.

Childcare programs operate with both direct and indirect expenses.

Direct expenses include:
- Meals and snacks
- Learning materials
- Cleaning supplies
- Equipment

Indirect expenses often include:
- Rent or mortgage
- Utilities
- Insurance
- Licensing fees
- Maintenance
- Administrative costs

For programs with staff, payroll becomes one of the largest expenses.

There are also costs related to training, compliance, and professional development. Even time itself has value. Long working hours must be considered as part of the cost of operating the business.

When all of these factors are included, the true cost of childcare becomes clear.

Pricing should reflect the full picture—not just the most visible expenses.

Building Profit Into the Model

One of the most important concepts for childcare providers to understand is that revenue and profit are not the same.

Revenue is the total amount collected. Profit is what remains after expenses.

A program can generate significant revenue and still struggle financially if pricing is not aligned with actual costs.

For example, a program with ten children paying $150 per week generates $1,500 weekly, or approximately $6,000 per month.

After expenses—rent, food, supplies, utilities, and insurance—the remaining amount may be significantly lower.

Now consider the same program charging $200 per week.

Weekly revenue increases to $2,000, and monthly revenue rises to approximately $8,000. With similar expenses, the provider now has more flexibility to cover costs, pay themselves appropriately, and reinvest into the program.

The difference is not just income.

It is sustainability.

Profit is not optional. It must be built into the pricing model from the beginning.

Without profit, a business cannot grow or maintain stability.

Creating a Sustainable Pricing Strategy

A strong pricing strategy begins with clarity.

Providers must calculate total monthly expenses, including both direct and indirect costs. From there, they determine how much revenue is required to cover expenses while also generating profit.

Enrollment capacity plays a key role.

Smaller programs may require higher rates per child, while larger programs may distribute costs across more enrollments.

Market research is also important.

Understanding local pricing helps providers stay competitive, but it should not dictate their entire strategy. Competing solely on price often leads to underpricing, while competing on quality and structure creates long-term value.

Confidence is essential.

Families are not simply paying for supervision. They are investing in a safe, structured environment where their children are supported and guided through critical stages of development.

Communicating Value to Families

Pricing is not just about numbers—it is about perception.

Families are more likely to accept tuition rates when they understand the value behind them.

Clear communication helps parents recognize the structure, safety, and professionalism within the program.

When providers explain their policies, routines, and expectations, they demonstrate that their program is organized and intentional.

Consistency is key.

When all families are charged the same rates and policies are applied equally, it creates fairness and trust.

Over time, this consistency strengthens the program's reputation.

Families who value quality care are willing to invest in environments that are stable, reliable, and well-managed.

A Shift in Mindset

For many providers, pricing requires a shift in perspective.

Instead of viewing tuition as a sensitive topic, it must be understood as a foundational part of the business.

Pricing decisions affect:
- Daily operations
- Financial stability
- Program quality
- Long-term growth

When pricing is set correctly, it supports the entire program.

When it is set incorrectly, it creates ongoing challenges that become harder to fix over time.

Childcare is a profession that requires responsibility, skill, and dedication.

The pricing of a childcare program should reflect that reality.

The Core Principle

At its core, pricing comes down to one essential truth:

If your business is not financially stable, it cannot continue to serve children at the level they deserve.

Charging appropriately is not selfish.

It is responsible.

Because when your business is strong, your program becomes more stable, your environment improves, and the children in your care benefit the most.

And in childcare, that is what matters most.

Chapter Seven

Policies That Protect Your Program

One of the biggest differences between a childcare program that struggles and one that runs smoothly is not just passion, experience, or even enrollment.

It is structure.

And at the center of that structure are policies.

Policies are not just paperwork. They are the foundation that holds your program together when situations become difficult, emotional, or unpredictable. Without them, even the most caring provider can become overwhelmed—constantly reacting instead of leading.

Many providers avoid creating strong policies in the beginning because they do not want to seem too strict. They want families to feel comfortable. They want to be liked. They want to be flexible.

But over time, that flexibility often turns into confusion.

Pick-up times begin to stretch. Payments come in late. Expectations become unclear. What started as an effort to be understanding slowly becomes a daily source of stress.

Policies are not there to create distance between you and families.

They are there to create clarity.

When expectations are clear from the beginning, everyone understands how the program operates. Families know their responsibilities, and providers are able to lead with confidence instead of hesitation.

A well-structured program is not built on constant explanations.

It is built on systems that already define how things are done.

Enrollment Agreements and Setting the Tone

The relationship between a childcare provider and a family begins long before the first day a child walks through the door.

It begins with the enrollment process.

An enrollment agreement is more than a form—it is the first opportunity to establish expectations and communicate how your program operates.

This document should clearly outline the terms of care. It should define what families can expect from you and what you expect from them in return. When done correctly, it sets the tone for the entire relationship.

Many providers rush through this step.

They focus on filling spots quickly and assume they can explain details later if issues arise.

This often leads to misunderstandings.

When expectations are not clearly written and agreed upon from the beginning, it becomes difficult to enforce them later. Conversations that should be simple become uncomfortable because there is no documented agreement to reference.

A strong enrollment agreement removes that uncertainty.

It creates a shared understanding that protects both the provider and the family. It allows you to refer back to a clear standard rather than relying on memory or verbal conversations.

Most importantly, it establishes professionalism.

Families are more likely to respect a program that operates with structure. It shows that you take your role seriously and that the environment their child is entering is organized and intentional.

Tuition Policies and Financial Consistency

One of the most sensitive areas in childcare is payment.

Providers often hesitate to enforce strict tuition policies because they understand that families may face financial challenges. They want to be supportive and avoid tension.

However, unclear payment expectations quickly become one of the biggest sources of stress in a childcare program.

Without structure, providers may find themselves:
- Chasing payments
- Making repeated exceptions
- Adjusting expectations constantly

This affects both finances and peace of mind.

A strong tuition policy should clearly define:
- When payments are due
- How payments should be made
- What happens if payments are late

It should remove all guesswork.

Consistency is essential.

When all families are held to the same standard, it creates fairness and predictability. There is no need for ongoing negotiation or individual arrangements that become difficult to manage.

It is important to remember:

Tuition is not just a fee.

It is what allows your program to operate.

It supports your environment, your materials, and your time.

When payments are consistent, your program is stable. When they are not, everything else begins to feel uncertain.

Clear tuition policies protect your ability to provide quality care without financial stress.

Late Pick-Up
Policies and Respecting Time

Time is one of the most valuable resources a childcare provider has.

Long days are already part of the profession. When those days are extended due to late pick-ups, exhaustion and frustration quickly follow.

Without a clear late pick-up policy, it becomes difficult to address this issue consistently.

A late pick-up policy establishes a firm boundary.

It defines:
- Your closing time
- Fees for late arrivals
- Consequences for repeated occurrences

This policy is not about punishment.

It is about accountability.

When expectations are clear, families are more likely to plan accordingly. They understand that your time is structured and that extending care affects the entire program.

Respecting time is essential for maintaining balance.

Policies that protect your time also protect your well-being.

Illness Policies and Protecting Health

Childcare environments naturally bring children into close contact with one another.

Without clear guidelines, illness can spread quickly.

An illness policy protects both the children in your care and the stability of your program.

This policy should define:
- When children must stay home
- Symptoms that require exclusion
- When children can return

It should also address what happens if a child becomes ill during the day.

Without structure, providers may feel pressured to accept children who are not well.

While the intention may be to help, the impact can be significant.

One sick child can affect multiple families and staff members.

An illness policy removes emotional decision-making.

It creates a clear standard that can be applied consistently.

Discipline Policies and Consistent Guidance

Every childcare program must have a clear approach to discipline.

Children are learning how to express emotions, manage behavior, and interact with others.

Guidance is a natural part of that process.

Without a defined discipline policy, responses can become inconsistent.

A strong policy focuses on:
- Guidance
- Redirection
- Teaching appropriate behavior

Consistency is key.

Children feel more secure when expectations are clear and responses are predictable.

This policy also creates alignment with families.

When parents understand your approach, it strengthens consistency between home and childcare.

Discipline, when handled correctly, becomes a tool for growth—not conflict.

Parent Communication and Expectations

Communication is essential in any childcare program.

Families want updates. Providers need to share information. Relationships depend on clarity.

Without boundaries, however, communication can become overwhelming.

Some parents may expect constant updates. Others may reach out at all hours.

A communication policy defines:

- How communication happens
- When communication happens
- What response times look like

This structure allows providers to remain professional without becoming overwhelmed.

When expectations are clear, families are more likely to respect them.

Clear communication builds trust—without sacrificing boundaries.

Structure Creates Stability

At the heart of every successful childcare program is structure.

Policies are not about removing compassion.

They are about creating stability.

Without structure, providers are forced to make decisions in the moment—often under pressure.

With structure, decisions are already defined.

Policies create a framework that:

- Reduces stress

- Prevents confusion

- Supports daily operations

Families benefit as well.

They know what to expect. They feel confident in the environment. They trust the program.

Leading with Confidence

Establishing policies requires confidence.

It means setting expectations and standing by them—even when it feels uncomfortable at first.

Providers without policies often feel like they are constantly adjusting and reacting.

Providers with structure are able to lead.

Over time, confidence grows.

What once felt strict becomes normal.

What once felt uncomfortable becomes necessary.

The Role of
Policies In Long-Term Success

Childcare is not just about daily care.

It is about building a program that can operate consistently over time.

Policies make that possible.

They protect:
- Your time
- Your income
- Your energy
- Your environment

Without policies, even the most passionate provider will struggle.

With policies, the program becomes sustainable.

The Core Principle

At its core, this chapter comes down to one truth:

Clear policies create stable programs.

They are not about control.

They are about protection.

They protect your business, your peace, and the children who depend on you every single day.

Common Mistakes That Cost Childcare Providers Time, Money And Peace

Many childcare providers don't fail because they don't care…

They fail because they were never shown how to run this like a real business.

Before you move forward, you need to understand what's holding most providers back.

1. Underpricing Your Services

This is one of the biggest mistakes in childcare.

You set your rates based on what feels affordable, what others are charging, or fear of losing families.

Instead of what it actually costs to run your business.

The result:

You work long hours

You stay fully booked

But you're still not making real money

Being busy is not the same as being profitable.

2. No Policies or Weak Policies

Many providers try to be flexible, but what they create instead is confusion.

Without strong policies:

Parents pay late

Pick-ups are inconsistent

Expectations are unclear

You feel stressed and overwhelmed

Policies do not push families away.
They protect your business.

3. No Structure

Running a childcare program without structure leads to chaos.

No clear schedule, systems, organization, or expectations.

The result:
Constant stress

Unpredictable days

Burnout

Children need structure.

Your business does too.

4. Trying to Figure It Out Alone

Most providers enter childcare with passion but no real guidance.

So they Google everything, copy others, and learn through trial and error.

That trial and error becomes expensive.

Time lost

Money lost

Energy drained

You don't need to guess your way through this.

5. Running Childcare Like Babysitting Instead of a Business

This is the difference between struggling and succeeding.

If you don't track your numbers, enforce policies, build systems, and lead with structure, your business will always feel unstable.

Childcare is not babysitting.

It is a structured business.

The Real Truth

If you see yourself in any of these, you are not alone.

Most providers start this way.

But the ones who succeed

Chapter Eight

Daily Operations & Systems

Creating Structure in Your Day-to-Day Program

One of the biggest differences between a childcare program that feels chaotic and one that runs smoothly is not the number of children, the size of the space, or even the level of experience.

It is structure.

Daily operations are what bring your program to life. They determine how your day flows, how children transition from one activity to the next, and how manageable your workload feels.

Without clear systems, even a small program can feel overwhelming.

With structure, even a full program can feel organized and controlled.

Why Daily Structure Matters

Children thrive in environments where they know what to expect.

Routine creates a sense of security. It helps children understand what comes next, reduces behavioral challenges, and supports their overall development.

But structure is not just for the children.

It is also for you.

A clear daily system:
- Reduces stress
- Improves time management
- Creates consistency
- Allows you to stay in control of your program

When your day is structured, you are not constantly making decisions in the moment.

You are following a plan.

A Typical Day in Childcare

While every program is different, most successful childcare programs follow a consistent daily rhythm.

A structured day might look like this:

6:00 AM – 8:00 AM: Arrival & Free Play

Children arrive, settle in, and begin their day with calm, supervised activities.

8:00 AM – 9:00 AM: Breakfast

Meals are served at a consistent time, followed by cleanup and preparation for the day.

9:00 AM – 11:00 AM: Learning & Activities

This may include structured learning, group activities, or guided play.

11:00 AM – 12:00 PM: Outdoor Play / Movement

Children engage in physical activity and fresh air.

12:00 PM – 1:00 PM: Lunch

A consistent meal routine followed by cleanup.

1:00 PM – 3:00 PM: Nap / Quiet Time

Rest time for children to recharge.

3:00 PM – 4:00 PM: Snack

A light meal and transition back into activity.

4:00 PM – 6:00 PM: Free Play & Pick-Up

Children wind down while parents arrive for pick-up.

This structure creates flow.

It allows the day to move smoothly without constant interruptions or confusion.

Managing Transitions

Transitions are often where the most challenges occur.

Moving from one activity to another can create frustration, especially for younger children.

Clear transitions reduce stress.

This includes:
- Giving children warnings before changing activities
- Using consistent routines for meals and cleanup
- Keeping transitions calm and organized

When transitions are predictable, children adjust more easily.

And your day becomes more manageable.

Classroom Structure and Environment

Your physical environment plays a major role in your daily operations.

A well-organized space allows children to move safely and independently.

Consider:

- Defined areas for play, learning, eating, and rest
- Easy access to materials
- Clear boundaries within the space

When everything has a place, your program feels more controlled.

Disorganization leads to confusion.

Organization supports structure.

Systems That Keep You Organized

Daily operations are not just about schedules.

They are also about systems.

Strong programs have systems for:

- Attendance tracking

- Meal planning
- Cleaning routines
- Supply organization
- Communication with parents

These systems reduce the need to constantly think about what needs to be done.

They create consistency.

And consistency creates stability.

Why Routine Creates Stability

Routine is not about being rigid.

It is about being reliable.

When your program operates on a consistent routine:
- Children feel secure
- Parents feel confident
- You feel in control

Without routine, every day feels different.

With routine, your program becomes predictable.
And in childcare, predictability is powerful.

Bringing It All Together

Daily operations are what turn your childcare program from an idea into a functioning system.

They shape how your program feels, how it operates, and how manageable it becomes over time.

You do not need a perfect schedule.

You need a consistent one.

Because in childcare, structure does more than organize your day.

It creates stability.

Part III

Growth and Success

Chapter Nine

How to Get Enrollments

Building a Childcare Program That Fills and Stays Full

One of the most common questions new childcare providers ask is simple:

How do I get children enrolled?

It is a valid question.

Because without enrollment, there is no business.

But what many providers do not realize is that enrollment is not just about marketing.

It is about trust.

Enrollment Starts With Perception

Families are not just choosing a childcare provider.

They are choosing a place where their child will spend a significant part of their day.

That decision is emotional.

Before a parent ever contacts you, they are forming an opinion based on what they see.

This includes:

- Your online presence
- Your communication
- Your environment
- Your professionalism

First impressions matter.

And in childcare, they matter quickly.

The Power of Word of Mouth

The strongest form of marketing in childcare is not advertising.

It is recommendation.

When a parent tells another parent that they trust you, it carries weight that no post or flyer can match.

Word of mouth is built through:

- Consistency
- Care
- Communication

- Professionalism

Happy families talk.

And those conversations lead to new enrollments.

Using Social Media the Right Way

Social media is a tool, but it should be used with intention.

It is not about posting constantly.

It is about showing:
- Your environment
- Your structure
- Your daily routines
- Your professionalism

Parents want to see what their child's experience will look like.

Clear, simple content builds confidence.

Tours and First Impressions

The tour is one of the most important steps in the enrollment process.

This is where parents decide whether they feel comfortable moving forward.

During a tour:

- Be clear about your policies
- Show your structure
- Walk them through your daily routine
- Answer questions with confidence

Parents are not just listening to what you say.

They are observing how you operate.

Closing the Enrollment

Many providers struggle at this stage because they hesitate.

They present information, but do not guide the decision.

Confidence matters.

If a family is a good fit, it is okay to move forward clearly.

Let them know the next steps.

Provide enrollment information.

Give them a clear path to secure their spot.

Clarity leads to action.

Building Trust Over Time

Enrollment is not just about filling spots.

It is about keeping them filled.

Families stay when they feel:
- Safe
- Respected
- Confident in your program

Trust is built daily.

Through consistency, communication, and structure.

Enrollment Is a Result, Not a Strategy

The most important thing to understand is this:

Enrollment is not something you chase.

It is something you attract.

When your program is:
- Structured
- Professional

- Consistent
- Trustworthy

Families notice.

And when they notice, they enroll.

Bringing It All Together

Getting enrollments is not about doing more.

It is about doing the right things consistently.

When you focus on:
- Building trust
- Maintaining structure
- Communicating clearly

Your program begins to grow naturally.

And growth that happens naturally is often the most stable.

Chapter Ten

Building Trust With Families

One of the most important factors that will determine whether your childcare program grows or struggles is not just your location, your pricing, or even your marketing.

It is trust.

Families are not simply choosing a service when they enroll their children. They are placing their children in someone else's care—often for long hours each day. That decision is deeply emotional. It is personal. And it is not made lightly.

A parent can like your program, appreciate your environment, and even agree with your policies—but if they do not trust you, they will hesitate.

And hesitation is enough to stop enrollment.

On the other hand, when trust is present, everything changes.

Parents feel comfortable. They feel confident. They refer other families. They stay longer. They become advocates for your program without being asked.

Trust is not something you can advertise.

It is something you build through your actions, your consistency, and the way you show up every day.

And in childcare, trust is what drives growth.

How Word of Mouth Really Works

Many providers focus heavily on flyers, social media posts, or online listings to grow enrollment.

While those tools can help, they are not what sustain a childcare business long term.

The strongest form of marketing in childcare has always been word of mouth.

When a parent tells another parent, "You can trust her with your child," that carries more weight than any advertisement ever could.

It is not just a recommendation.

It is reassurance.

Word of mouth is built on real experiences.

It comes from:

- How children are treated
- How parents are communicated with
- How consistent the program feels over time

Families talk to each other. They share experiences in their workplaces, neighborhoods, and communities.

If those experiences are positive, your program grows naturally.

If they are not, growth becomes difficult—no matter how much effort you put into marketing.

This is why trust must be built intentionally.

Every interaction matters. Every conversation matters. Every decision contributes to how families speak about your program when you are not in the room.

Your Reputation in the Community

Your childcare program does not exist in isolation.

It becomes part of a larger community—and over time, that community forms an opinion about what your program represents.

Reputation is not built overnight.
It is built through consistency.

When families see that your program is organized, respectful, and reliable, they begin to associate your name with those qualities. They recognize your standard.

This reputation extends beyond the families currently enrolled.

Neighbors observe your program. Other providers hear about your work. Parents searching for care hear your name in conversations.

Reputation grows quietly—but it carries weight.

It can open doors or create barriers depending on how your program is perceived.

Building a strong reputation requires attention to detail.

It shows in:

- How you communicate
- How you handle challenges
- How you maintain your environment
- How you treat every child

People may not see everything that happens inside your program—but they will always see the results.

Relationships With Parents Matter

At the heart of every successful childcare program is a strong relationship between the provider and the families they serve.

These relationships are built over time through communication, respect, and consistency.

Parents want to feel that their child is not just another number.

They want to know their child is seen, understood, and cared for as an individual.

When providers take the time to build genuine relationships, parents notice.

Often, it is the small moments that matter most.

Greeting parents warmly at drop-off.

Sharing updates about their child's day.

Remembering details about a child's personality or progress.

These moments create connection.

And connection builds trust.

However, building relationships does not mean removing boundaries.

Professionalism must always remain.

Families should feel valued—but they should also understand that the program operates with structure.

A strong relationship is not built on overextending yourself.

It is built on mutual respect.

Creating a Family-Like Environment

Many successful childcare programs are described as having a "family feel."

This does not mean removing structure or professionalism.

It means creating an environment where children feel safe and families feel connected.

When families feel like they are part of something meaningful, they become more invested in the program.

They communicate openly.

They support the provider.

They show understanding during challenges.

Children benefit from this as well.

They thrive in environments where relationships are consistent and where they feel secure and valued.

When families experience this level of connection, they do not just stay.

They refer others.

They become part of the growth of your program.

Trust Is Built Through Consistency

Trust is not built in a single moment.

It is built over time through consistent actions.

Parents observe more than providers often realize.

They notice:

- Whether your program starts on time
- Whether policies are followed
- Whether communication remains clear

Consistency creates predictability.

And predictability creates comfort.

When parents know what to expect, they feel confident leaving their children in your care.

Inconsistent programs create uncertainty.

When rules change or expectations shift, trust begins to weaken.

Consistency removes that doubt.

It shows that your program is structured, reliable, and intentional.

Handling Challenges the Right Way

Every childcare program will face challenges.

Children may struggle with behavior.

Parents may have concerns.

Difficult conversations will arise.

How you handle these moments matters.

Avoiding issues or responding emotionally can damage trust.

Addressing concerns with professionalism, clarity, and respect strengthens it.

Parents do not expect perfection.

They expect honesty, communication, and accountability.

When providers handle challenges with care and confidence, it reassures families that their children are in capable hands.

Even difficult situations can strengthen relationships when handled correctly.

Trust and Enrollment Growth

Trust is directly connected to enrollment.

Families who trust your program are more likely to stay long term. They are also more likely to refer others.

This creates a natural cycle of growth.

Instead of constantly searching for new enrollments, your program begins to attract families organically.

Referrals come with built-in trust.

Parents who are referred often arrive already confident in their decision because they have heard positive experiences from someone they trust.

This type of growth is more stable.

It leads to:

- Stronger relationships
- Longer enrollment
- A more consistent program

A Foundation That Cannot Be Replaced

Many factors contribute to the success of a childcare business.

Marketing, pricing, location, and structure all matter.

But none of them can replace trust.

Trust is the foundation that holds everything together.

Without it, growth becomes difficult to maintain.

With it, everything else becomes easier to build.

Families are not just looking for childcare.

They are looking for a place where their children will be safe, supported, and genuinely cared for.

When they find that, they stay.

And when they stay, your program grows.

Building trust takes time, intention, and consistency.

But once it is established, it becomes one of the most powerful assets your childcare program will ever have.

Chapter Eleven

The Income Potential of Childcare

There is a belief that has followed the childcare industry for years, and it has shaped how many providers think about their work.

The belief is simple:

There is no real money in childcare.

It is often repeated so casually that many people accept it as fact before they even begin. Providers enter the industry expecting to struggle financially, assuming that passion is the reward and income will always be limited.

But that belief is not entirely true.

The reality is more nuanced.

Childcare can absolutely generate high, stable income. It can grow into a six-figure business. It can expand into multiple programs and create long-term financial security.

At the same time, many providers never experience that level of success.

The difference is not in the industry itself. The difference is in how the business is structured, how it is managed, and how intentionally it is grown.

Understanding the income potential of childcare requires a shift from a survival mindset to a business mindset.

It requires seeing childcare not only as a service, but as a system that can be built, strengthened, and scaled over time.

How Small Home Daycares Reach Six Figures

One of the most surprising realities of the childcare industry is that even small, home-based programs can generate six-figure annual revenue.

At first, this may seem unrealistic. Many people assume that only large childcare centers can reach that level of income. But when enrollment and pricing are structured correctly, the numbers begin to tell a different story.

Consider a home daycare that is licensed to care for twelve children.

If the weekly tuition rate is set at $220 per child, the program generates $2,640 each week. Over the course of a month, that becomes $10,560. Projected across a full year, the total reaches $126,720 in revenue.

This example is not based on extreme pricing or unrealistic enrollment. It reflects a properly structured program operating at capacity with consistent tuition.

What makes this possible is not just the number of children enrolled. It is the combination of enrollment, pricing, and consistency.

Providers who maintain full enrollment, enforce clear tuition policies, and manage expenses effectively can build strong financial foundations even within smaller programs.

However, it is important to understand the distinction between revenue and profit.

Generating six figures in revenue does not automatically mean the provider is taking home six figures in personal income. Expenses such as food, supplies, utilities, licensing, and assistant wages must still be considered.

Even so, a well-managed home daycare can provide a strong and sustainable income when pricing is aligned with the true cost of operating the program.

How Childcare
Centers Generate Higher Revenue

While home-based programs have strong earning potential, childcare centers operate on a different scale.

Centers are designed to serve larger numbers of children, which significantly increases overall revenue potential.

A childcare center with sixty enrolled children, each paying $200 per week, generates $12,000 weekly. Over a month, that becomes $48,000. Over the course of a year, revenue reaches $576,000.

These numbers highlight the impact of scale.

With multiple classrooms, extended hours, and a structured staffing system, centers are able to serve more families and generate higher income.

However, higher revenue also comes with higher expenses.

Payroll becomes one of the largest costs in a childcare center. Staff members must be hired, trained, and scheduled according to licensing ratios. Rent or mortgage payments for commercial space are typically higher than operating from a home. Utilities, insurance, maintenance, and supplies also increase.

Because of this, the focus for childcare centers cannot be on revenue alone.

It must also be on operational efficiency.

When a center is properly structured, higher revenue can support a team, maintain quality standards, and still produce strong profit margins.

But without structure, higher enrollment alone does not guarantee financial success.

Scaling Enrollment the Right Way

Growth in childcare is often measured by enrollment.

More children usually means more revenue. But scaling enrollment must be done carefully if the quality of care is going to remain strong.

Filling spots quickly may feel like the goal, but sustainable growth requires planning.

Providers must consider capacity, staffing, and their ability to maintain consistent care as enrollment increases. Overcrowding or overextending staff can lead to burnout and a decline in quality.

Successful providers scale with intention.

They monitor enrollment patterns, maintain waiting lists, and ensure that each new child added to the program fits within the structure they have created.

Scaling also requires strong policies and systems.

As enrollment grows, communication, scheduling, and daily operations must remain organized. Without that structure, growth can quickly become chaotic.

Growth should feel controlled, not overwhelming.

When enrollment is scaled properly, it strengthens the program instead of putting pressure on it.

Hiring Staff and Building a Team

At a certain point, growth requires support.

For many providers, that means hiring staff.

Bringing in additional team members allows the program to expand capacity, maintain appropriate ratios, and provide more structured care throughout the day.

However, hiring staff introduces a new layer of responsibility.

Providers must shift from managing only children to also managing people. This includes hiring, training, scheduling, communication, and ensuring that staff members align with the program's values and standards.

The quality of your team directly affects the quality of your program.

Parents are not only trusting you with their children. They are trusting the entire environment you have created, including the adults who interact with their children each day.

Hiring should be done carefully.

It is not just about filling positions quickly. It is about finding people who understand the importance of care, structure, and professionalism.

Once a strong team is in place, the provider can begin stepping into a leadership role instead of handling every task personally.

That shift is essential for long-term growth.

Expanding Programs for Greater Opportunity

Beyond increasing enrollment and hiring staff, many childcare providers expand by offering additional services.

This may include after-school programs, summer camps, or specialized learning programs for specific age groups.

Expansion allows providers to serve a wider range of families while creating additional revenue streams.

For example, an after-school program can operate during hours when full-day childcare is not in session. Summer programs can fill gaps when school is out, helping maintain more consistent income throughout the year.

Some providers also expand by opening additional locations.

This level of growth requires strong systems, experienced staff, and clear leadership. It is not simply about repeating the same model. It is about ensuring that every location maintains the same standards and structure.

Expansion should always be approached with preparation.

Growth without structure leads to inconsistency. Growth supported by strong systems creates stability.

The Difference Between Working in the Business and Building the Business

One of the most important shifts a childcare provider can make is moving from working in the business to building the business.

In the early stages, providers are involved in every part of daily operations. They care for children, prepare meals, clean, communicate with parents, and manage administrative tasks.

As the program grows, it becomes necessary to step back from some of those daily responsibilities and focus on the larger structure of the business.

This includes planning for growth, managing finances, developing systems, and leading a team.

Providers who remain involved in every task often find it difficult to expand.

Providers who build systems and delegate responsibilities create space for growth.

This shift does not happen overnight, but it is essential for reaching higher levels of income and stability.

A New Perspective on Childcare Income

The belief that there is no money in childcare often comes from programs that were never structured for financial success.

Underpricing, weak policies, and poor planning can limit income regardless of enrollment.

But when childcare is approached as a structured business, the potential becomes clear.

Income is not determined by the industry alone.

It is determined by how the business is built.

Providers who understand their numbers, maintain consistent enrollment, and operate with clear systems are able to create programs that are both impactful and financially sustainable.

Childcare is meaningful work.

It requires dedication, patience, and responsibility.

But it can also be profitable work when approached with the right structure.
The goal is not only to care for children.

It is to build a program that supports both the families being served and the provider leading it.

When those two elements come together, childcare becomes more than a service.

It becomes a business with real potential.

What You Can Realistically
Earn In Childcare

One of the biggest misconceptions about childcare is that it cannot be profitable.

That is simply not true.

Childcare can become a strong, stable, and income-producing business when it is structured correctly, priced correctly, and operated with intention.

The income potential will depend on your business model, your location, your rates, your expenses, and how well you manage your program.

But the truth is this:

Childcare has real income potential.

Many providers enter the industry thinking small. They assume childcare is only enough to get by.

In reality, a well-run childcare business can create consistent monthly revenue and long-term financial stability.

Home Daycare Income Example

If you care for 6 children and charge $200 per week per child:

6 children × $200 per week = $1,200 per week
$1,200 per week × 4 weeks = $4,800 per month

That equals:

$4,800 per month
$57,600 per year

If you charge $250 per week:

6 children × $250 per week = $1,500 per week
$1,500 per week × 4 weeks = $6,000 per month

That equals:

$6,000 per month
$72,000 per year

Larger Home Daycare Example

If you care for 10 children and charge $225 per week:

10 children × $225 per week = $2,250 per week
$2,250 per week × 4 weeks = $9,000 per month

That equals:

$9,000 per month

$108,000 per year

Childcare Center Income Example

If a center enrolls 40 children at $220 per week:

40 children × $220 per week = $8,800 per week

$8,800 per week × 4 weeks = $35,200 per month

That equals:

$35,200 per month

$422,400 per year

Larger Center Example

If a center enrolls 60 children at $250 per week:

60 children × $250 per week = $15,000 per week

$15,000 per week × 4 weeks = $60,000 per month

That equals:

$60,000 per month

$720,000 per year

Revenue Is Not the Same as Profit

Revenue is the total money your business brings in.

Profit is what remains after expenses are paid.

Your goal is not just to fill spots.

Your goal is to build a childcare business that is priced correctly, structured correctly, and profitable after expenses.

The Real Truth

The childcare industry can absolutely create real income.

But profitability does not happen by accident.

It happens when you:

choose the right business model

understand your numbers

set tuition with intention

protect your revenue with strong policies

operate with structure instead of emotion

Childcare is not just a passion.

It is not just supervision.

And it is not just extra money.

When built correctly, childcare can become a serious business, a stable source of income, and a long-term legacy.

Chapter Twelve

The STARS Method™

Framework for Building a Successful Childcare Program

By now, you understand that building a childcare program requires more than good intentions.

It requires structure.

It requires consistency.

And it requires a clear understanding of how each part of your program works together.

Many providers enter the childcare industry with passion, but without a system. They try to figure things out as they go, adjusting day by day, reacting to situations instead of leading with intention.

Over time, this approach creates stress, inconsistency, and instability.

What separates programs that struggle from those that succeed is not effort alone. It is structure.

Through my own journey—building, learning, and growing within the childcare industry—I developed a framework that brings clarity to that structure.

I call it the STARS Method™.

This method represents the five core areas that every successful childcare program must have in place. When these areas are aligned, your program becomes stable, organized, and sustainable.

When they are not, challenges begin to show.

S – Structure

Structure is the foundation of your entire program.

It defines how your business operates on a daily basis and sets the tone for everything that happens within your environment.

Structure includes your policies, your routines, your systems, and your expectations.

It determines how drop-off and pick-up are handled.
How your day flows from one activity to the next.
How you respond to situations when they arise.

Without structure, your program becomes reactive. Each day feels unpredictable, and decisions are made in the moment rather than guided by a clear system.

With structure, everything becomes more manageable.

Children benefit from predictable routines.

Families understand what to expect.

And you are able to lead your program with clarity instead of confusion.

Structure is not something that develops over time on its own.

It is something you intentionally create.

T – Training

Training is what prepares you to operate your program correctly and confidently.

Childcare is a profession that requires knowledge. It is not something that can rely solely on instinct or experience alone.

Understanding child development, safety procedures, licensing requirements, and effective communication is essential.

Training allows you to handle situations with confidence rather than hesitation.

It also becomes critical as your program grows.

If you bring on staff, they must be trained to follow the same standards and expectations you have established. Consistency within your program depends on everyone operating from the same understanding.

When training is clear, your program runs smoothly.

When it is not, confusion begins to take over.

Training is not a one-time event.

It is an ongoing process that supports the growth and quality of your program.

A – Accountability

Accountability is what keeps your program consistent.

Many providers understand what they should be doing, but struggle with enforcing it.

They create policies, but do not follow through.

They set expectations, but make frequent exceptions.

They avoid difficult conversations in an effort to maintain comfort.

Over time, this weakens the structure of the program.

Accountability requires you to stand by what you have established.

It means enforcing your policies consistently.

It means maintaining clear financial expectations.

It means holding both yourself and your families to the same standards.

This is not about being inflexible or unkind.

It is about being consistent.

When accountability is present, your program becomes predictable and professional.

Families know what to expect, and respect the structure you have created.

R – Relationships

Childcare is built on trust, and trust is built through relationships.

Families are placing their children in your care. That level of responsibility requires more than just meeting basic expectations.

It requires connection.

Relationships are developed through consistent communication, respect, and reliability.

Parents want to feel confident that their child is safe, supported, and understood. They want to know that they can rely on you, not just for care, but for stability.

Strong relationships create long-term enrollment.

They lead to referrals.
They build your reputation within the community.

However, relationships must exist within structure.

Being warm and supportive does not mean removing boundaries.

In fact, clear boundaries often strengthen trust, because they show that your program is organized and intentional.

The goal is to create an environment where families feel both comfortable and confident.

S – Sustainability

Sustainability is what allows your program to continue long term.

Many childcare businesses begin with strong intentions but struggle to maintain stability over time.

This often happens when the business is not built with sustainability in mind.

Sustainability includes proper pricing, consistent enrollment, managing expenses, and creating systems that support your daily operations.

It also includes protecting your own well-being.

Burnout is common in childcare when providers operate without structure or financial stability. Long hours, inconsistent income, and constant stress can make the work feel overwhelming.

A sustainable program creates balance.

It allows you to provide quality care while also maintaining a stable and manageable business.

It supports both the children you serve and the life you are building for yourself.

Bringing the STARS Method Together

Each part of the STARS Method serves a purpose, but it is the combination of all five that creates a strong program.

Structure provides direction.
Training builds knowledge.
Accountability maintains consistency.
Relationships create trust.
Sustainability ensures long-term success.

When one area is missing, challenges begin to appear.

When all areas are aligned, your program becomes stable, predictable, and professional.

Applying the STARS Method

You do not need to perfect everything at once.

Start by identifying where you currently are.

Look at your program and ask yourself:

- Where do I need more structure?
- What areas require more training or understanding?
- Am I being consistent in what I enforce?
- How strong are my relationships with families?
- Is my program built to sustain itself long term?

These questions create awareness.

From there, you can begin making adjustments.

Small improvements in each area will lead to significant progress over time.

A Different Way of Thinking

The STARS Method is more than a framework.

It is a shift in perspective.

It moves you from simply running a childcare program to intentionally building a structured business.

It helps you lead with clarity instead of reacting to situations as they arise.

And it provides a path that you can follow as your program grows.

Childcare is meaningful work.

But when it is built with structure, intention, and consistency, it becomes something more.

It becomes stable.

It becomes sustainable.

And it becomes successful.

Part IV
My Journey

Chapter Thirteen

Why I Never Gave Up

There are moments in life that change you in ways no one can see from the outside.

Moments that reshape how you think, how you feel, and how you move through the world.

For some people, those moments happen slowly over time. For others, they arrive all at once—without warning—leaving you to figure out how to stand again when everything inside of you feels broken.

My journey in childcare was never just about business.

It was built through moments that tested me in ways I never expected. Moments that forced me to decide whether I was going to stop… or keep going, even when it felt like I had nothing left.

There were days when I was tired in a way that sleep could not fix. Days when I questioned everything. Days when I felt completely alone, carrying responsibilities that no one else could fully understand.

But even in those moments, I did not give up.

Not because it was easy, but because I had a reason that was bigger than how I felt.

Living Through Loss

Losing a child is something that changes you forever.

There are no words that can fully explain that kind of pain. It is not something you move on from. It is something you learn to carry—one day at a time.

When my son passed away, a part of me changed in a way that could never return to what it was before.

The dreams I had, the plans I imagined, the life I thought I would be living—all shifted in a moment.

Grief does not follow a schedule.

Some days it is quiet, sitting in the background. Other days, it feels overwhelming, as if it just happened all over again.

And yet, life does not stop.

Responsibilities remain. Work continues. People still depend on you, even when you feel like you are trying to hold yourself together.

There were days when simply showing up felt like the hardest thing I had ever done.

Days when I had to care for other children while carrying my own pain silently.

Days when I had to be strong for everyone else… even when I did not feel strong at all.

But somehow, I kept going.

Not because I had all the answers, but because I chose to move forward—even if it was one small step at a time.

The Weight of Doing It Alone

Being a single mother comes with a level of responsibility that never turns off.

There is no one to hand things off to when you are tired. No one to step in when you need a break.

Everything falls on you.

Every decision. Every bill. Every responsibility.

And when you are building a childcare program at the same time, that weight can feel even heavier.

There were moments when I felt like I was balancing everything on my own—trying to hold together my personal life while also running a program that required my full attention.

It was not just about showing up.

It was about showing up consistently.

Children depend on routine. Families depend on stability. A childcare program does not pause because you are going through something difficult.

So I learned how to keep going—even when things felt overwhelming.

I learned how to push through exhaustion, manage responsibilities, and continue building something… even when I felt like I was starting from a place of struggle.

It was not perfect.

There were mistakes. There were hard days. There were moments when I questioned whether I could continue.

But every time I thought about giving up, I thought about why I started.

The Loneliness No One Talks About

There is a kind of loneliness that comes with building something on your own.

People see the progress. They see the growth. They see the success.

But they do not always see the quiet moments behind it.

The late nights spent trying to figure things out. The pressure of making decisions without guidance. The feeling of carrying everything without someone to share it with.

When you are responsible for everything, it can feel isolating.

There were times when I wished I had more support. Times when I wanted someone to understand what I was going through without having to explain it.

But I also realized something important.

Even in those moments of loneliness, I was building strength.

I was learning how to depend on myself. How to make decisions. How to keep going—even when things felt uncertain.

That strength became part of the foundation of everything I built.

Choosing to Keep Going

There is always a moment when you have to decide whether you are going to continue or stop.

For me, that moment did not come just once.

It came again and again.

Moments when things felt too heavy. Moments when I was exhausted. Moments when I questioned whether all the effort was worth it.

But every time, I made the same decision.

I chose to keep going.

Not because it was easy, but because I understood that what I was building mattered.

It mattered for my family.
It mattered for the children in my care.

It mattered for the future I was creating.

Giving up would have meant walking away from something that had purpose.

And I could not do that.

Finding Purpose in the Work

Childcare is more than a job.

It is a responsibility.

It is about creating an environment where children feel safe, supported, and valued.

Through everything I experienced, that purpose became even clearer.

I knew what it felt like to need support. To need stability. To need someone to care.

And I wanted to create a space where children would always have that.

My experiences shaped how I approached my program.

They made me more intentional. More protective. More focused on creating an environment where children were not just supervised—but truly cared for.

That purpose gave me something to hold on to.

It reminded me why I started… and why I needed to keep going.

Strength Built Over Time

Strength does not always look the way people expect it to.

It is not always loud. It is not always visible.

Sometimes, strength is simply continuing to show up.

It is getting through the day when you feel like you have nothing left. It is making decisions when you are unsure. It is continuing to build something—even when the process feels difficult.

Over time, those small moments of persistence add up.

They create resilience.

They shape the person you become.

Looking back, I can see how every challenge, every loss, and every difficult moment contributed to the strength I have today.

Not because those moments were easy—but because I chose to keep going through them.

A Message for Those Who Feel Like Giving Up

There will be moments in your journey when you feel like stopping.

Moments when things feel too hard. Moments when you question whether you are capable.

That feeling is not a sign that you are failing.

It is part of the process.

You do not have to have everything figured out.

You do not have to move forward in big steps.

Sometimes, continuing simply means taking the next step in front of you.

What matters is that you do not stop.

When I look back on everything I have been through, I realize something clearly.

Giving up was never really an option.

Not because I always felt strong—but because I had a reason to keep going.

My experiences shaped me.

They challenged me. They tested me. They pushed me in ways I never expected.

But they also gave me clarity.

They showed me what mattered.

They helped me build something that was not just about business—but about purpose.

I did not give up because I understood that what I was building was bigger than the challenges I faced along the way.

And because of that…
I kept going.
One day at a time.

Chapter Fourteen

Opening My Childcare Center

There are moments in life when you realize you have stepped into something bigger than anything you have ever done before.

Moments where everything you have worked for, struggled through, and sacrificed for begins to take shape in a way that feels real.

Opening my childcare center was one of those moments.

It did not happen overnight. It did not come easily. It was built through years of experience, mistakes, lessons, and growth.

By the time I reached that point, I had already spent years in childcare. I had learned how to manage daily operations, support families, and create an environment where children could thrive.

But opening a center was different.

It required a new level of commitment. A new level of vision. A new level of responsibility.

It meant taking everything I had learned and expanding it into something greater—something that could serve more families, support more children, and create a lasting impact within my community.

The Decision to Expand

The decision to open a childcare center did not come from convenience.

It came from purpose.

Over time, I began to notice the gaps in childcare around me. I saw families struggling to find quality care. I saw programs lacking structure. I saw environments where children were not receiving the level of attention and support they deserved.

I knew what it felt like to search for a place where your child would be safe, cared for, and valued.

I had lived that experience.

And I knew I could create something better.

The decision to expand was not just about growth.

It was about responsibility.

It was about stepping into a role where I could build an environment that reflected everything I believed childcare should be.

But making that decision was only the beginning.

The Licensing Journey

Opening a childcare center requires patience, attention to detail, and persistence.

Licensing is not something that can be rushed.

There are requirements to meet, standards to follow, and inspections designed to ensure that programs are safe and prepared to operate. Every part of the process exists to protect children—and that was something I took seriously.

The journey required time.

There were documents to complete, regulations to understand, and expectations to meet at every level. There were moments when the process felt overwhelming, when it seemed like there was always one more step to take.

But I understood why it mattered.

Every requirement was part of building something safe, structured, and ready to serve families the right way.

So I stayed committed.

I paid attention to the details. I made sure everything was in place. I did not cut corners because I knew what I was building needed to be done right from the beginning.

When the licensing process was complete, it was more than just approval.

It was confirmation that the vision I had worked toward was now becoming reality.

Building Something From the Ground Up

Opening my center meant building something from the ground up.

That came with its own challenges.

There were decisions about the layout, the environment, the daily structure, and how everything would operate. Every detail mattered.

I wanted the space to feel intentional.

Not just a place where children would be watched, but a place where they would be cared for, supported, and allowed to grow.

I thought about how classrooms would function, how routines would flow, and how the environment would support both children and staff.

Everything needed to align with the standards I had developed over the years.

I was not just opening a center.

I was creating a reflection of everything I believed childcare should be.

The Grand Opening

The day of the grand opening is something I will never forget.

After everything it took to get there, seeing the doors open for the first time felt like stepping into a new chapter.

It was more than a business milestone.

It was a moment of resilience.

It represented every challenge I had overcome, every lesson I had learned, and every decision I had made to keep going.

Standing there, looking at what had been created, I felt a sense of accomplishment that is difficult to put into words.

Not because it was perfect—

But because it was real.

The Ribbon-Cutting Moment

One of the most powerful parts of that day was the ribbon-cutting.

Having the mayor present to recognize the opening of the center was a moment I will always remember.

It was a reminder that what I had built was not only impacting individual families, but also contributing to the community.

Moments like that do not happen by accident.

They come from years of dedication, from showing up consistently, and from believing in what you are building—even when the process feels difficult.

Standing there, I reflected on the journey.

From the early days of figuring everything out, to the challenges I faced, to the decision to expand and build something bigger.

It all led to that moment.

And in that moment, I understood that everything I had been through had a purpose.

A Different Kind of Responsibility

Opening a childcare center changes your role.

It is no longer just about managing a small program.

It becomes about leading a team, maintaining a larger structure, and ensuring that everything operates consistently.

The responsibility grows.

Families trust you with their children. Staff members depend on your leadership. The program relies on your ability to maintain direction and stability.

It requires a shift in mindset.

You move from doing everything yourself to building systems that allow the program to run effectively.

You focus on leadership, training, and creating an environment where everyone understands their role.

It is not easy.

But it is necessary for growth.

What This Moment Meant

Opening my childcare center was more than a milestone.

It was proof that something meaningful can be built from the ground up.

It was a reminder that the challenges I faced were not wasted.

They prepared me.

They shaped me.

They helped me grow into the person I needed to become to lead at that level.

Growth is not just about expansion.

It is about stepping into new responsibilities, learning how to lead, and continuing to build with intention.

A Message for Those Who Want More

If you are at the beginning of your journey, it may feel like moments like this are far away.

It may feel like opening a center is something that only happens for certain people.

But it starts with a decision.

A decision to take your work seriously.
A decision to build structure.
A decision to keep going—even when it feels hard.

Growth does not happen all at once.

It happens step by step.

The same way I started.
The same way I learned.
The same way I built over time.

Looking Ahead

Opening the center was not the end of my journey.

It was the beginning of a new phase.

A phase that required continued growth, continued learning, and continued commitment.

Because building something is one thing.

Maintaining it, growing it, and leading it over time is another.

That is where the real work continues.

But standing in that moment, seeing everything come together, I knew one thing for certain.

Everything I had been through had led me there.

And it was only the beginning.

Conclusion

If I Can Do It, So Can You

There is a moment that comes for almost every person who considers starting something new.

It is quiet, but it is powerful.

It sounds like a question:

What if I am not ready?

That question stops more people than failure ever will.

It creates hesitation before the journey even begins. It causes people to second-guess their ability, their timing, and their worth.

And in childcare, that question shows up in many different ways:

What if I do not have enough experience?
What if I do not have enough money?
What if I make a mistake?
What if I fail?

Those thoughts are real. They are honest.

But they are also the very things that keep people from building something that could change their life—and the lives of others.

If there is one thing my journey has taught me, it is this:

You do not have to have everything figured out to begin.

You just have to be willing to start—and committed enough to keep going.

It Was Never Perfect

When I began, I did not have a perfect plan.

I did not have all the answers. I did not have a step-by-step roadmap that guaranteed everything would work out.

What I had was a reason.

A reason rooted in my experiences, my challenges, and my desire to create something better for children.

That reason carried me through moments of uncertainty.

Because the truth is, there will always be uncertainty.

There will always be things you do not know yet. There will always be situations that require you to learn, adjust, and grow. Waiting for everything to be perfect is another way of not starting at all.

Growth does not happen in stillness.

It happens in motion.

It happens when you take the first step—even when you are unsure of the outcome.

Courage Is Required

Starting a childcare program takes courage.

It is not just about caring for children. It is about stepping into responsibility. It is about deciding that you are capable of building something that other families will trust.

Courage does not mean you are not afraid.

It means you move forward anyway.

There will be moments when doubt shows up. Moments when things feel bigger than you expected. Moments when you question your decision.

That is part of the process.

The difference between those who build something meaningful and those who stop is not the absence of fear.

It is the decision to keep going in spite of it.

Structure Is What Sustains You

Passion may bring you into childcare, but structure is what keeps you there.

Without structure, everything begins to feel overwhelming. Decisions become reactive. Days feel unpredictable. Stress builds.

Structure creates stability.

It gives your program direction. It allows you to operate with clarity instead of confusion. It supports you on the days when things feel difficult.

The systems you put in place, the policies you enforce, and the standards you maintain all work together to create a foundation you can rely on.

Structure is not something you add later.

It is something you build from the beginning.

Leadership Changes Everything

At some point in your journey, you will realize that childcare is not just about what you do.

It is about how you lead.

Leadership shows up in your decisions. It shows up in how you handle challenges. It shows up in how you guide both children and the people around you.

You do not have to be perfect to be a leader.

You just have to be consistent.

Children need stability. Families need trust. Staff need direction.

When you lead with clarity, your program reflects that.

When you lead with uncertainty, your program feels that too.

Leadership is something you grow into.

It develops over time through experience, through mistakes, and through the willingness to keep learning.

Persistence Is What Carries You Through

There will be moments when things feel hard.

Moments when you are tired. Moments when you feel like you are putting in effort without seeing immediate results. Moments when challenges seem to come one after another.

This is where persistence matters.

Success in childcare is not built overnight.

It is built through consistency.

Through showing up day after day. Through continuing to improve. Through learning from what does not work and adjusting as you go.

Persistence is not about never struggling.

It is about not stopping.

Every step you take forward—no matter how small—moves you closer to the program you are building.

Your Story Has Value

One of the things that holds many people back is the belief that their story is not enough.

They compare themselves to others. They feel like they do not have the right background, the right experience, or the right circumstances.

But the truth is:

Your story matters.

Your experiences shape how you care. They shape how you connect with children and families. They shape the environment you create.

What you have been through does not disqualify you.

It strengthens you.

There are families who will connect with your story. Who will trust you because of your experiences. Who will feel safe knowing that you understand what it means to care.

You do not have to be like anyone else.

You just have to be consistent in who you are and what you are building.

It Will Not Always Be Easy

There is a part of this journey that must be said honestly:

It will not always be easy.

There will be long days. There will be challenges. There will be moments when you feel stretched in ways you did not expect.

But difficulty does not mean something is wrong.

It means you are building something real.

Every meaningful path comes with challenges.

What matters is how you respond to them.

When you begin to see challenges as part of the process instead of a sign to stop, everything begins to shift.

You become stronger. More capable. More confident.

When I look back at everything I have been through, I do not see a perfect journey.

I see growth.
I see struggle.
I see decisions to keep going when it would have been easier to stop.

I see lessons. Mistakes. Strength built over time.

And I realize something important:

If I was able to build something through all of that…
then it is possible for you too.

Not because our journeys will look the same—

But because the same principles apply.

Courage to start.
Structure to sustain.
Leadership to guide.
Persistence to continue.

Those are the things that make the difference.
The Decision Is Yours

At this point, you have what you need to think differently.

You understand that childcare is more than a passion.

It is a responsibility.
It is a business.
It is an opportunity to create something meaningful.

Now the next step is yours.

You can move forward.

Or you can stay where you are and continue to wonder what could have been.

There is no perfect moment to begin.

There is only the moment you decide.

Moving Forward

You do not have to take the entire journey at once.

You just have to take the next step.

Start where you are.
Use what you have.
Learn what you need along the way.

And continue to build.

Because the truth is simple:

If I can do it…
so can you.

Closing Section

Next Steps

If you have made it this far, something inside of you is already shifting.

You are no longer looking at childcare the same way you did before. You are beginning to see it for what it truly is—not just a way to care for children, but an opportunity to build something meaningful, structured, and impactful.

And now, the question becomes simple:

What are you going to do with what you have learned?

Information alone does not create change.

Action does.

Everything shared in this book was meant to give you clarity—to help you see what is possible and to prepare you for what it takes to build a childcare program the right way.

But understanding is only the beginning.

Execution is what moves you forward.

Start With the Right Foundation

If you are serious about starting your childcare program the right way, begin with the right guidance.

I've created resources to help you move forward with clarity instead of confusion.

Start with the free guide.

Then go deeper with the workbook, templates, and step-by-step support designed to help you actually build your program—not just think about it.

These tools are designed to help you:
- avoid common mistakes
- stay organized
- and move forward with confidence

You Don't Have to Do This Alone

There is a difference between trying to figure everything out on your own and having guidance from someone who has already done it.

If you want support, structure, and direction as you build your childcare business, mentorship is available.

You don't have to struggle through every step.

You can build this the right way from the beginning.

Take the First Step

Starting can feel overwhelming.

But you don't need to do everything at once.

You just need to take the next step.

Start where you are.
Use what you have.
Learn as you go.

Progress is built through action.

Your Journey Starts Here

You have everything you need to begin.

Now it's your move.

If you're ready to take the next step, you can access all of my resources here:
www.stan.store/valeriechester

Inside, you'll find:

- your free guide
- workbooks
- templates
- and mentorship

Everything designed to help you start, build, and grow your childcare business the right way.

The opportunity is in front of you.

All you have to do…

is begin.

About the Author

Valerie is a childcare business owner, mentor, and advocate with over 15 years of experience in the childcare industry.

What began as a personal journey grew into a mission to create safe, structured, and nurturing environments for children—while helping other providers build successful and sustainable childcare programs.

Her path into childcare was not traditional. It was shaped by real-life experiences that required her to grow, adapt, and lead with purpose. As a single mother, Valerie built her childcare business from the ground up, learning firsthand what it takes to start, manage, and expand a program while balancing real-life responsibilities.

Over the years, she has successfully operated childcare programs and opened her own childcare center—an accomplishment that reflects her resilience, dedication, and commitment to doing things the right way.

Valerie is known for her strong belief that childcare is more than babysitting.

She teaches that childcare must be structured, professional, and intentional in order to truly serve children and families. Her approach combines real-world experience with proven systems that help providers avoid costly mistakes and build programs that are both impactful and financially sustainable.

Through her work, she has helped aspiring and established childcare providers gain clarity, implement structure, and grow their programs with confidence.

Her mission is simple but powerful:

To protect children, support families, and help childcare providers build programs that operate with purpose, structure, and long-term success.

This book is a reflection of her journey, her lessons, and her commitment to helping others succeed in the childcare industry.

To learn more, access resources, or work with Valerie, visit:
www.stan.store/valeriechester

For more business tips and daily insights, follow:
@valeriechestermentor
@valeriebusinessmentor